HOPE IS NOT A STRATEGY

Frameworks for
Simplifying the Chaos of Work & Life

Chuck Scothon

First published by Dog Ear Publishing
4010 W. 86th Street, Ste H
Indianapolis, IN 46268
www.dogearpublishing.net

ISBN: 978-1-4575-3009-8

Library of Congress Control Number: has been applied for

This book is printed on acid-free paper.

Printed in the United States of America

Prologue

I have been working on this book for a long time. I am not sure why I started a book, but the fact that it is cheaper than therapy is probably the best explanation. It may also be that I have always spoken in catch phrases and used pithy little ideas to get teams that I have worked with to align quickly. I have also begun to realize how these simple thoughts not only aligned teams of people, but, more importantly, allowed me to be less reactive and more in control of most situations. Also, after resigning a senior-level position at Mattel with no clear plan on what my next step was career-wise, telling people I was working on a book sounded better than telling them I had no clear idea of what I was planning to do with my life, so a book gets started, and here is the result.

I will admit that when I started this project, my focus was on how the ideas I was prepared to share were useful and could be applied to work. However, as I have written and re-written (and re-written again) the various drafts of the book, I have come to realize that these thoughts or phrases can also be applied to everyday life. I sincerely hope you find the frameworks helpful with work, life, or maybe both. What I can say with certainty is that these frameworks have changed the way I think of virtually everything, both at work and at home. Hopefully you will feel the same way as you continue through the chapters and that, at the very least, you find this to be a quick, fun, and interesting read.

First, a little background about me:

I have been married for the last eighteen years to a beautiful wife who was crazy enough to move from Florida to Buffalo, New York, something everyone suggests says "true love." Twelve years ago we were blessed with a gorgeous baby girl that we named Gabriella. To be honest, life has never been the same. The subtitle of this book is about dealing with the "chaos of life," and there is no doubt that children and marriage contribute to that chaos, making me realize that chaos is not a bad thing, but something that everyone has in their life and something to embrace.

From a work perspective, I have spent the last twenty-five years working in the business world, mostly in toys. My roles have ranged from entry-level marketing jobs in smaller companies to senior-level general management positions at Mattel, the world's largest toy company. It has been an amazing career. Like all careers, it has been filled with exceptional highs and demoralizing lows, but through it all, the greatest thing about my work has been the ability to work in an industry that is focused on entertaining children in a way that is healthy, inspiring, and exciting. I am sure you remember a favorite toy you had as a child; having the opportunity to be involved in creating and developing the toys that will create that sort of memory for a child growing up today is tremendously rewarding.

When I look back at all the roles I have had, from my first job, at which I learned to braid hair for a line of fashion horses, or my last job as the Head of US Marketing for all brands at Mattel, each position and role required an unwavering focus on one thing—inspiring kids to have fun and helping parents to understand how toys help their children develop and grow. I won't pretend that all of the toys and brands I worked on always achieved that goal (I worked on and launched some very bad toys over the last twenty-five years), but I can say that when the toy was right, when it struck that perfect match between what moms and kids wanted and had an ability to inspire their imaginations, magic happened and Christmas morning was a much happier place in many homes.

I didn't set out to spend most of my career in the toy business. I knew that I wanted to be in marketing, but beyond that, I let my interests and the opportunities present themselves. I was lucky. Every two years, I was presented with new roles and new opportunities that made the same company feel new again. Truth be told, I never thought I would get a chance to run global brands like Fisher Price or Barbie, but I did, and both experiences were the most amazing times I have ever had in business.

As the SVP of Marketing for Fisher Price, I had the opportunity to oversee the re-invention of the brand both from a product point of view and in terms of how we as a brand engaged and spoke to moms. These changes created significant growth for Fisher Price and helped to change the preschool toy business. The challenge was quite different when I took over leadership of Barbie, arguably the best-known toy brand anywhere in the world. After many years of decline, the focus was on getting the brand back to its roots, raising the bar on the toys being made, and ensuring that Barbie stood for something positive and aspirational for girls of all ages. I will speak more to the challenges and the accomplishments during this assignment in later chapters, but for now, I will say that it was while running the Barbie brand that the first framework I will share ("Hope is Not a Strategy") became a reality.

While the two roles referenced earlier were very different and required different things from me and the teams with whom I worked, there was also a commonality between Barbie and Fisher Price. Specifically, both roles required teams of people to come together, deal with complex situations rapidly, and establish action plans that would result in better performance. The common thing I used in both roles were "frameworks," or ways of thinking, talking, and acting that helped to align the huge groups of people that work on these brands every day. Marketers, designers, engineers...there are hundreds of people behind these brands that bring them to life. My job, simply put, was to get them to start thinking, acting, and feeling the same goals, the same vision, and the same purpose. Once we were all aligned, I simply had to get out of the way and let the talent of the people take over.

This sounds easy, but it is very hard to do when an organizational culture is strong and well-established, as it was with Barbie and Fisher Price. Looking back, I now realize that the frameworks I used in those roles, and that I write about in this book, helped to accelerate change, drive a common alignment among disparate functions, and, ultimately, simplify the organizational "chaos." There is nothing complex or unique in most of the thoughts I will share here. It was *how* and *when* I used them that I now realize was so critical. These frameworks provided a great way to harness the power of people and teams while removing the "noise" that is present when faced with tough challenges. The fact is that if you cannot simplify what needs to be done and align people quickly, chaos ensues and "office politics" becomes the norm.

I will use the word *simplify* a lot in this book, and I do so intentionally because in today's business world, and life in general, people are overwhelmed. There are too many e-mails to read and respond to, too many people providing input, and too much information available to think and rethink everything. Companies continually downsize, restructure, and re-organize with the goal of getting more work done with less people. How many times has someone said to you, "It is not about doing more with less; it's about working smarter"? It is a great theory, and it's usually said by someone who "doesn't do the work," but it is the reality of today's workplace and something that everyone in a leadership role must embrace. This "more with less" theory is truly the new standard.

"Hope is not a strategy" is the first framework I will share, but also the underlying and central theme to all the frameworks that follow. Simply put, you cannot "hope" your way out of issues. Figuring out ways to make sure you are not depending upon hope as your solution will make your life better and more satisfying. Again, it's not easy, but it is critical to becoming more effective.

The idea in the first chapter is a foundational thought that I will occasionally bring back throughout the book to show how it influences many of the other frameworks. I should also add that "hope is not a strategy" does not mean hope is unimportant—in fact, it's a critical emotion and something that must always be present at work or in life. You, your teams, and your organization need hope. It's central to why we try and try and try again when faced with adversity. However, as the phrase states, while it's important, it cannot be the core or central element of a solution to solve an important issue.

CHAPTER 1

Hope is Not a Strategy

This is my favorite saying in the entire book, and I start here because it sets a foundation for how I have changed my approach to daily life. "Hope is not a strategy" is a simple thought, but one that has great meaning to me. I also believe it can apply to virtually any situation, in or out of work, once you both embrace the idea and figure out how to apply it yourself.

A little background:

"Hope is not a strategy" came to me in the middle of the night after what can only be described as the worst year of my career. I was leading the girls' division of Mattel as the SVP and General

Manager, and after my first fourteen months, I felt like this was the year when we would really turn things around. Instead, it was a year in which every plan we started did not achieve what we thought, a year in which my team and I missed virtually every measurement that we were expected to achieve. Be it our sales goals, our profit goals, or our spending targets—you name it, we missed it. I had worked for almost twenty years and never had a year like this. Adding insult to injury, I'd agreed with our goals when they were established. They were not unrealistic or unachievable, and they were not handed down from some corporate group. They were my goals, and I believed we would meet them.

Looking back at that year, many factors could be blamed. Without question, there were many things outside of our control that affected our plans. In hindsight, though, we only made it worse because of our strategy for the year, which turned out to be *hope*. *Hope* wasn't our written plan, nor did we realize at the time that it had become our *de facto* strategy, but as you read more of this chapter, you will see how it became the foundation of everything that went wrong.

I realized that hope had become our strategy a few days before a management offsite meeting that I was leading with the other key leaders of my team. People have called it my *Jerry McGuire* moment (the moment in that movie when he writes a manifesto in the middle of the night), but I simply call it a moment of insight driven by sheer terror. You see, we had just wrapped up the horrible year I referenced earlier and were working on plans for the next year. We were busy revising our plans on the fly, given the recently delivered poor results, and we were headed into my staff meeting offsite to plan for the next year. As I began preparing, I really didn't know what to say to this leadership team. I knew these people were talented, I knew they were not reflective of the results that we had just posted (I was secretly hoping I wasn't, either), and I knew that we needed a different approach, given how the previous year had finished, but before I could even begin to think about what we needed to do differently, it was evident that the entire team, myself included, needed to better understand what had gone wrong.

Leading up to the offsite meeting, I had heard members at all levels of the division discussing the year and pointing to various parts of the company or outside influences that could be blamed for the performance. The commentary wasn't wrong, as some of the external issues definitely had a negative impact, but I also knew there was something deeper, something more fundamental that had created this "perfect storm" of horrible performance. I could feel it, almost taste it, but I was struggling to put it into words. We all knew there were a lot of things contributing to the poor performance of the previous year, but I kept asking myself one question: "Was there one thing that caused or amplified the issues and created such poor performance?"

It hit me at 4:00 one morning. I awoke with great clarity regarding how I could articulate this issue to the leadership team and, ultimately, to the organization. At the core, it was clear that the Mattel Girls Division, under my leadership, had spent the year making decisions (or not making decisions) by sticking to our original plan and ignoring reality. Ultimately, I didn't ask the right questions or force the right conversations that would require that we deal with the reality of the situation. Instead, the organization and its leader (me) ignored reality and simply kept going in the same direction despite underperforming on virtually every indicator that could be evaluated. We were not making difficult decisions early enough, we were not addressing organizational problems that were affecting our work, and we were not stepping back to evaluate whether we should change course. Instead, we had unknowingly implemented a strategy of hope—an unwritten, never talked about strategy, but one that certainly existed (even if we didn't realize it at the time). Even more absurd, we as a team had strategic plans, marketing plans, sales plans, spending budgets, and every other metric to evaluate how we were doing, and even though they weren't working, we stuck to them. We kept marching to the end, despite what both the numbers and reality were telling us. We were blindly moving forward, "hoping" things would improve.

I came to this conclusion at 4:00 a.m. It may not have been the best time to have such an epiphany, but this early morning time will help you get to the heart of the issue quickly and without distractions. Following are a few quick examples that came to me that morning that illustrated how hope had become our underlying guide:

I worked at Mattel, the world's number-one toy company and a company that has a product in virtually every household with kids. In this business, a company makes thousands of new toys each year. On any given day, you can see how your business is performing—every day, every week, every month, you can see what you sold and compare this to what you needed to sell to make your goals. It could be by item, by segment, by brand, by retailer, or in total. It didn't matter.

You could look at it any way you wanted and project how you were doing. Unfortunately, when the early results for the year started to come in at Mattel, we ignored them. Why? Because everyone, myself included, was convinced that "it is going to get better."

"Spring merchandise isn't selling well, but that's okay; we have a new fall line going in, and the fall line will be a lot better."

"Fall is starting slowly, but that's okay because we haven't kicked off TV advertising yet."

"TV just started, and sales still aren't performing, but that's okay because retail is slow and will pick up for the Christmas season."

I could go on and on, but you see the pattern. I kept hoping things would improve. Obviously, looking back, we all should have dug deeper to really understand the business issues and taken action, but for whatever reason, we had adopted a strategy of hope.

Another example in which hope had become our strategy is found by looking at how we managed the spending in our division. Division spending is always planned to align with our revenues, which is no surprise, not complicated, and probably exactly how you manage your own household budget. If more money comes in, you save or spend more. If less money comes in, you save or spend less. This is not complex; it is something I was taught very early in my life. In this year of hope, however, as sales kept falling, I didn't change our spending. I hoped that sales would get better, and since I knew our plans or strategies couldn't be the issue, I kept things going as originally budgeted. You see the sense of hope playing out here? Again, I saw the numbers and actual results, but I was not believing and reacting to the reality in front of me. I was too invested in our existing plans to really evaluate and make the necessary changes. As a result, when sales never materialized, we had truly missed every deliverable that mattered.

A final example of how this "Hope" strategy had an impact was found in how this hope was impacting our people and, more specifically, how the day-to-day work environment was preventing the teams from delivering great results. As stated earlier, Mattel designs and delivers thousands of new products each year. Throughout that year, there were times that the teams were truly energized. Typically, these times were framed around brainstorms. Everything about these brainstorms focused on creativity and inspiration, from the locations of the events to the people involved. As leaders, we knew of these moments of inspiration, remembered these events as truly energizing, and remarked about how these meetings were so inspiring, but looking back, those moments of inspiration were the exception, not the rule. The everyday company processes had squeezed the life and creativity out of our people instead of providing it to them. As a leadership team, we had talked about these issues before, but talk was all that we did. Instead of taking action, changing our processes, and making creative moments of inspiration a part of our everyday environment, we "hoped" it would get better.

There were many more examples, and I used a lot of them in a four-page "manifesto" that I shared with my leaders and the entire division, and which I now share with you.

Hope is not a strategy......

It has been two years since the reorganization of Mattel Brands and during that time, we have made many decisions that affected our brands, our people, the leadership of the division, and everything else in between. It has been a time of incredible change, mostly positive in terms of the way we work, but as we sit here today....at the tail end of 2007, I find myself asking what needs to change next? Too many people are working too hard for the results we are currently living.

When you look at the current state of the business, you'll hear that the recalls were horrible and how they have caused us to falter, you'll hear many reference how international is holding up or "at least doing OK" (although I would guess we don't really know why). We are also good at pointing to other outside influences and suggesting that there was nothing we could do. Two years ago it was Bratz, now it's HSM, Hannah, Littlest Pet Shop, etc. Who or what will be next...will it be us? We also look at our retailers and suggest that they just don't get it. To be honest, I know that I have engaged in each and every one of those conversations, excuses and reasons. Yet as I sit here today, I believe that we owe it to ourselves, our teams and to the entire organization to dig deeper, to talk more, and to get to the underlying issues....not the symptoms of the much bigger disease that is affecting all of us.

When I first arrived in El Segundo, I used a phrase at one of the first all hands meetings...."stop the madness". Well, we stopped part of it....but in the end, we haven't yet stopped or changed the things that must be changed for all of us to see the results of our hard work and our effort. It would be easy to sit here today, say 'stay the course', and hope that by next year the results would be different...well, I for one can no longer count on **hope** as a strategy. Instead we must **act**...**act** to change the things we think, we know, we believe, are inherently the issues. This is a divisional issue that starts with me. So, with conviction, here are the things that I believe we must address on all of our brands:

We are NOT inspiring anyone.....our consumers, our retailers, our internal partners, ourselves. If we were, the other issues would no longer be problems. SKU's would not be nearly as inefficient as they are now, trade support would not be lagging and we wouldn't be fighting over the last few feet or poor ad cuts. We hit it right occasionally, but not consistently and certainly not often enough considering how hard we are all working.

We continue to do things because we have always done them…..whether they were our best use of time or energy, we are more concerned with **not** doing something and wondering how we will cover the gap vs making a few things work like never before.

We seem to acknowledge our issues, but are we really doing anything about it….We talk about our schedules, yet we don't really change what we are doing to address our timelines, sku counts, start ups, etc.…..everyone knows the definition of insanity, so why are we doing the same things again and again?

We have become a commodity….. no different than diapers or formula. We have to provide better and greater clarity around the **benefits** we provide to girls of all ages.

So with those issues in front of us, let me lay out what I believe we need to do for 2008 and beyond…..

Inspire girls, moms, and ourselves …... This is unquestionably our #1 priority. Its needs to start with the 2008 marketing plans, that when combined with amazing product, will be how we inspire people, how we change from being viewed as a commodity to being considered a "gotta have".

Change behaviors…not words….. We need to identify the behaviors that are driving the madness and stop them…..from how much product we develop for spring and/or fall, to how much time we spend on each, from how much is mainline vs customized, to how many products/features we include….. "if it feels like a tough process, smells like a tough process, and is a tough process to make it through the "gauntlet" to get an item in the line", then that needs to change. Think about the energy coming out of the design offsite week and consider how we make that the norm, not the exception.

Honestly evaluate our time, our spend, and our priorities..... Not because I believe we spend too much, but because I believe we spend too much inefficiently and ineffectively. I believe that we can manage our business no differently than our personal budgets....we will spend what we have and we will figure out what we will do without if we don't have the money. I realize it sounds simple, and also realize its not.....the challenge will be for all of us to make the hard choices, consider what's important but not impactful and collectively make the calls on where to spend our time and money.

Benefits, not features.....Lastly, we need to focus on the benefits of our toys, not the features. I truly believe it's about our brand experience and we need to look at everything we are doing to insure that we are bringing something new to the party. Toys are an emotional purchase. Moms and girls buy toys because we connect with them emotionally and give them something they want, meaning a unique benefit.

In closing, this is a Mattel Girls issue and one that every one of us has a stake in going forward. This is not just a team issue or a management issue or a budgeting issue.....this is a behavioral issue. Remember the words I wrote earlier, I take full responsibility for where we sit and what we are doing. There is nothing in the '07 plans or results that I did not approve, implicitly or explicitly. However, with another difficult year, it would be irresponsible not to challenge and change things going forward. Finally, I truly believe in our people and our brands....together they can be the most powerful force in the toy industry if we really step back, change the way we operate, and unlock the potential of Mattel Girls.

Remember, **hope is not a strategy.**

Now you see the document that inspired this chapter. I am very proud to say that it had an amazing impact on the entire team, including both the leadership and its leader (me). "Hope is not a strategy" not only seemed to articulate what many were feeling, but couldn't or wouldn't say, but it also did something that turned out to be even more important than simply rehashing a bad year. "Hope is not a strategy" gave everyone in the division a way to question the existing plan at any point in time without attacking anyone personally in terms of how performance was tracking. The following year, I found myself in many meetings where the original strategy was in question and instead of saying, "The strategy was right or wrong" (which immediately puts the project owner on the defensive), someone from the team would say, "Well, you know, hope is not a strategy". Using this phrase was almost like screaming, "Stop! What are we doing?", which then created an opportunity for everyone to begin to discuss the facts and revisit whether anything needed to be re-evaluated. This moment of requiring everyone to ask if we were really being honest with ourselves created the chance to step back and look at what was going on, and then plan a path forward without finger-pointing or blame. As you can imagine, it became a powerful tool.

It transformed both the way I managed and, I like to think, the way the teams worked. Again, it is a simple thought, but this statement became powerful in that it jumpstarted important conversations and made all the difference in the morale of our people and teams. There is no question that since the manifesto moment, the Girls Division at Mattel has had tremendous success. I won't pretend that this statement or the document was the reason—there were simply too many talented and creative people working in this group for any single thing to be the reason for their success that year—but I also believe that the articulation of our struggles in a way that was non-threatening, all-encompassing, and not personal to anyone created a tipping point that helped change the way the team worked for the better. Ultimately, I believe it drove enough change within the culture to allow creativity and collaboration to thrive.

Finally, as you think about "Hope is not a strategy" and what it means for you, ask yourself if there are areas in which you might be running your life, your business, or your relationships on a strategy of hope. If you can identify an area where "hope" is the main plan to resolving an issue, immediately start to think about how you want that issue or part of your life to be resolved. Once you have a clear endgame in mind, begin taking actions to move toward that goal. You may need to alter plans based on how things start progressing, but you will start to feel significantly better just by taking action and no longer being reactive. Don't wait, and don't hope for resolution. Begin planning for it now. It can be terrifying to take the first step, but at least you're not "hoping" for something to change—you are changing it.

CHAPTER 2

"Are We Treating the Symptom or the Disease?"

This phrase sounds simple, but this is another key thought that took me a long time to understand and appreciate. I am sure that everyone has had situations in which two or more very smart people were making much more of a problem than they should have. You sit and listen, you watch as discussions take place that don't make sense, or you hear from others about circular arguments amongst team members, and you simply cannot understand why people are at such crossroads over such a simple topic. What I have found is that 95% of the time, when two smart people are arguing and disagreeing over something relatively small, you can almost guarantee that the argument has nothing do with the specifics being discussed. It's funny, but I find this idea truer every time I watch or become involved in a "small area" in which people find themselves unable to gain agreement. The discussion and lack of progress are symptoms of a much bigger disagreement over something more foundational. Whether it's the fundamental strategy of the project itself, objectives that are not aligned (and no one realizes it), or simply a lack of trust between the two folks working together, it's amazing how many big issues in the office are the result of something that is *not* about the topic being discussed. This focus on the wrong thing, the symptom instead of the disease, is at the core of this chapter, so let me try and provide a few examples to make this concept more concrete and clear:

Many times in the product development process, design and marketing would be at odds over a project. Despite having worked very closely for days or weeks on the idea, it was not unusual for these groups to reach a point where they could not resolve an issue. Arguments over whether an idea was good enough, whether the price was acceptable, or whether the feature was "fun enough" were common. As I spent time working to resolve the issue being discussed, the team usually agreed on many of the answers to questions posed to get to the bottom of things. What I learned over time, however, was that their disagreement or concern was usually not about the topic at hand, but something much more fundamental that was usually decided and resolved far earlier in the project or process. They were not misaligned on the current topic as much as they were misaligned on something far upstream and established at the beginning, such as the objective of the project. By asking two questions, it was amazing how quickly and consistently the core issue could be identified, and the entire conversation would change. Those questions are

(1) What is the problem we are solving for?

AND

(2) What is the endgame or vision for this project when it's complete?

I know these questions sound similar, but I have found that by getting answers to the questions above, it often exposed the fundamental issues upon which teams could not align/agree. They might agree on the upfront objective or strategy in theory, but never really agree in meaning. One side interprets things a certain way, the other side interprets it differently, and, suddenly, small differences in interpretation have manifested themselves into significant gaps within teams.

A visual example of this is drawing two lines leaving the same point, but only two degrees apart in their direction. At the beginning, there is not much disconnect; both lines appear to head in the same direction. As the line gets longer, the gap widens and the two lines pull apart. Teams and teamwork are very similar in that regard. Small differences that start early, if not corrected and regularly recalibrated, will become wide gaps later in a project, when you can least afford problems and disconnects. If you were to look at the big disconnect, the "symptom" is the big gap at the end, but the "disease" is the two degrees of disconnect at the beginning.

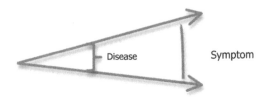

Going back to those two questions, asking the team both of these questions forces team members to agree on the issue or problem they are solving, as well as the end goal, and does not use "hope" as the solution to ensuring alignment. Once you have this alignment, everyone can look at the point at which the argument has been occurring and typically reconcile which side achieves the end result more effectively. Again, if it is about the endgame and solving a common problem, then staying focused on that and not worrying about the path to get there is dramatically more constructive.

Using this method of ensuring alignment at the beginning isn't tough, but it has taught me never to assume that I am aligned with anyone. Instead, I try and start critical meetings not with paper, but with a general statement about what the goal for the meeting is. If heads nod positively, we are good to go and all of us will be much more likely to stay aligned and move forward. If the nods don't come and I get something more akin to what I refer to as "the Labrador head turn" (puzzled looks with heads cocked slightly to the side), I make sure we spend time before moving onto the meeting agenda to get to the heart of what others think needs to be done and what they believe to be the end goal. There are times this can be frustrating, because it feels like you are not moving forward or that you are moving more slowly than you would like, but getting this alignment at the beginning is worth every moment you take to get it and will pay you back with dramatically greater speed and decision making later in the project or process.

Let me see if I can make this a little more "real." Think about your job. How many times have you had a meeting that seems to spin and churn, and it appears that people are confused? They want to spend time talking about topics that you think are not relevant or trying to revisit issues that are not on the agenda. I would suggest that what you are actually witnessing is a lack of alignment on what the end goal is and what the problem the team is working to resolve actually is. It becomes a spinning, churning dysfunctional meeting because the participants are all approaching the same topic differently and solving for different things. It is amazing how quickly you can change the paths of these train-wreck meetings by simply asking the two key questions: "What are we solving for?" and "What is our end goal?" Once everyone has to answer these questions, you will find out how each participant is approaching the topic and likely get to the heart of the disconnect.

As you face problems, make sure that you are focused on the underlying and fundamental issues and not spending all of your time and energy treating "symptoms." Treat the disease, and the symptoms will take care of themselves.

CHAPTER 3

If You Can't Fix It, Feature It

Okay, I'm not sure where this one started. It may have been in the first few years of working. I'm not even sure I recognized the theory or idea at the beginning, but over the last ten years, it has become something of a clear guiding light when things get difficult and I am trying to figure out what to do next. Let me see if I can articulate this in a simple way and then provide an example or two that may make it more real.

"If you can't fix it, feature it" is a framework that I use when faced with a problem. The problem can be with people, with processes, or with something being designed, built, or manufactured. At the heart of this philosophy, when you are faced with an issue, there are two options to resolving the problem. The first option is to do what you can to hide or work around the issue. The second option is to actually feature the problem. Don't try to cover it up or hide it, but make it a part of the design, the idea, the strategy, etc. It sounds insane, but if you put the big hairy issue in the center and acknowledge it, in all likelihood, it will not be the problem you expected it to be. Admittedly, putting the issue front and center sounds counterintuitive, but I have seen and experienced this method of problem solving, and it works miracles. I have also found that if it doesn't work, you probably have other issues with the idea, which means you are probably "hoping" for a positive resolution; as already discussed, hope is not a strategy or plan for resolving anything. As before, I will try and give you a few examples to see if they ring true.

I'll start with product design and how I have seen the thought of "if you can't fix it, feature it" apply many times. In toy design, you have a "parting line," or slight gap, where two pieces join together. This could be at the arm, the shoulder, or the hip on an action figure or doll or it could be two pieces coming together on an activity item—who knows where the line will be, but every toy has these, given the way they are made and how tooling is created to make them most efficiently. In the design of a toy, teams will spend an inordinate amount of time minimizing this parting line, perfecting a method to hide the gap, and, ultimately, getting the design just right, so that as you look at the sample, it will look great. In the toy business, you don't make just one sample. You need to make hundreds of thousands of the same item, and in toy manufacturing, it can be very expensive to hold every produced item to such a tolerance that you will never see the gap. While effort can and should be made to keep this gap consistent, small, and aesthetically pleasing, it will never disappear. No matter how hard you try, your problem isn't the parting line and minimizing it; your problem is the production process and holding the tolerance to such strict expectations. Therefore, when faced with these gaps, we learned to actually make them part of the design. During my time at Kenner Toys, in action figures, we would use these gaps within the look and paint operations of the action figures—don't try to avoid it, but use it to either make a natural color break or break up a single strong color. There was no single answer as to how we used it, but when we focused on using the gap instead of hiding it, the project could progress significantly quicker and more effectively. This focus on "featuring the gap" eliminated a lot of time spent making something "aesthetically perfect" in a first sample that the company could not reproduce consistently. Understand that as long as the gap didn't impact the way a child played with the toy, no seven year old was ever going to notice. Once we all realized that we could apply this framework to product design, we found that we could move more quickly, simplify areas that would normally be problematic, align with everyone on what was critically important, and move forward. Applying this theory has helped me to simplify the process of product development for teams that have worked for me and helped to either bring projects to conclusion more quickly or to realize that an idea was flawed from the beginning.

Another example of the "if you can't fix it, feature it" approach is related to people, and it helped me deal with a difficult PR situation facing Mattel. Specifically, my PR team and I found ourselves confronted by a reporter who had an angle on a story that was not going to be positive—at least as we understood her position. We started to fix the problem by trying to convince her it really wasn't a story, that it was old news, and that none of us were around for the era she wanted to discuss, but she was persistent and determined to run with the story, so we applied the "if you can't fix it, feature it" rule. We not only met with the reporter, but we facilitated conversations with people she might not have known about or had access to, but who did have very good awareness of the total story she was seeking. She met with all these folks, plus others, and because of this increased level of access, ultimately found that there was not a story worth writing. By trying not to "fix" the issue or avoid the story, we "featured it," opening ourselves up to share what we knew about the topic. It felt risky at the time, but in hindsight, it made all the sense in the world. Because we had removed the "veil of secrecy" that was making the story seem so intriguing to the reporter and had worked with the reporter, she ended up having the same takeaway that we did, that there really wasn't a story, after all.

I look back on that example with the reporter and am not surprised at the results. Today, you would hear it discussed and spoken about as "transparency." In its simplest form, it's really about acknowledging upfront any issues, short-comings, or concerns that might be present in a situation and allowing these to become a part of the dialogue. Instead of spending an inordinate amount of time "hiding" or minimizing some-thing, you can spend that same amount of time and energy (or less) on the areas that truly mat-ter and make a difference for positive reasons. This shift in your focus will allow you and the team to accomplish far more than originally planned because you are focused on making something work instead of trying to hide an issue.

A final example in which I have applied this framework or thought process is in dealing with employees that are seen to be a performance problem. Time and time again, I have found that when I am struggling with the value or performance of an employee, he is also struggling with his job. He may be struggling for a completely different reason, but he is almost always frustrated and very aware that there is an issue. He is typically not happy at work, usually confused about expectations management has about him, is getting negative feedback at work, and, without question, is stressed about the situation getting worse. The problem employee is likely spending an inordinate amount of time trying to "hide" the issues instead of focusing on what is really needed to improve.

In these situations, I have found that the first time you truly engage an employee with a direct and focused conversation about there being a problem and about their performance being an issue, this conversation almost always leads to a series of conversations that are different and more meaningful than previous efforts. I may have previously tried to discuss the concerns, but, ultimately, until I "feature" the problem directly, it never seems to progress to a point of mutual resolution. Maybe I was being too polite, maybe I was not stating the issue directly, or maybe the employee simply didn't want to hear the feedback at the time. Whatever the reason, it hadn't worked. After a direct conversation, however, by featuring the issue, the conversation has started a much more difficult conversation that is necessary, helpful, and almost always effective at resolving the core issue. As I stated before, the employee is likely struggling and aware there is an issue. By "featuring the issue," you provide this employee with an opportunity to engage in the facts and understand the perception about her performance. It will also give you an opportunity to understand her perception of the situation, which is also very valuable when it comes to working out a satisfactory solution. Bringing it out into the open is actually a huge step for both sides toward resolving the issue. Regardless of the resolution, bringing the issue out in the open keeps both parties moving forward instead of always looking back, trying to figure out what is not working, and hoping (there it is again) that the problem will resolve itself.

I offer one final challenge before moving beyond this chapter: Think about a problem you are struggling with and, instead of trying to fix it, feature it. It might be work-related or personal— it truly doesn't matter. Accept the problem as a given and instead of minimizing it, determine how you will live with it. Living with it doesn't mean forgetting about it; it simply means that instead of letting it consume you, you accept it and determine what or how you will handle things knowing you cannot change the situation yourself. I will be stunned if you don't find it amazingly powerful. By accepting the issue, you will unlock not only a sense of relief, but also a level of creativity and freedom that is energizing. I realize this is not the easiest thing to do, but when you truly accept the problem, you are well on your way to solving it.

CHAPTER 4

The Power of Three

I am certain this concept goes way beyond me and is likely written up with a lot more perspective, thought, and value than I may give it in this chapter. That said, if there is one rule I have applied in virtually every situation I have confronted at work, it is to approach challenges through a simple framework that I call the "Power of Three."

The theory behind this framework is that when faced with a significant challenge or problem, look at the situation and do everything possible to break it down and segment it into three "buckets," or areas of focus. By reframing your thoughts into three distinct areas, you actually begin to think strategically instead of tactically about what you are facing and how to best address the situation. Without framing your thoughts into the three segments or areas of focus, it is likely that you are getting caught up in the detail, the minutia, and may not be seeing the larger picture.

I have applied the Power of Three framework when working with and trying to lead teams. I have used the approach to help plan core business strategies or to create my personal goals. I have also used the same thinking to frame up and focus how I communicate. Be it small group discussions or presentations to large audiences, this mechanism truly helps to construct an easy-to-understand dialogue between you and the audience. This concept of the power of three is really a "forcing" mechanism that requires you to keep looking and looking at situations until you think big enough, clearly enough, and simply enough to be able to see the entire situation.

I often think about situations in business in which I am truly challenged. In working to resolve those challenges, most of us will create a "To Do" list. Unfortunately, my experience suggests that the "To Do" list is created with so many tasks that it becomes overwhelming and too daunting to complete. There is simply too much that needs to be done. Each task is usually important, but if constructed only by thinking tactically, there is a very good chance that the bigger issue or issues have not been identified. Plus, on truly complex issues, there is a high likelihood that many of the "to dos" are interdependent, but this interdependence isn't seen clearly because we only see the list, not the commonalities between the tasks. It is critical to push the thinking to a higher level, to see these interdependencies, and to ensure that the list of tasks has truly captured everything that needs to be done. This is the only way to truly solve the problem in its entirety.

This Power of Three framework seems to work because people can and do remember three things very well. I believe that most people forget or get overwhelmed by lists that are longer.

By structuring a challenge and an action plan in three segments, it seems like this challenge or task can be tackled and resolved even if there are many tasks within each segment. A list that is twenty tasks long will feel too big and too difficult and will be highly demotivating. A list of three strategic issues that must be resolved, even with twenty tasks within those three areas, seems to be much more achievable.

I am sure there is science behind this theory that provides a much better explanation to this thought than my anecdotal observations. Time and again, I find this theory holds true. For example, have you ever been asked to remember four priorities? What about that grocery list of four things? I have found in these circumstances that I can typically recall three priorities or items from the list, and there is always that one that I cannot remember. To better illustrate the Power of Three idea, here are specific ways I have used it beyond the "To Do" list:

Let's start with business leadership. I have found consistently that virtually every business challenge can and should be looked through a framework of *People*, *Process*, and *Product*. This framework forces me to evaluate whether I have the right team (the people); whether they are working together in a good, healthy, constructive manner (the process); and what the goal or output is that they are trying to create (the product). Interestingly, I have also found that by asking my teams to work and think this way, it changes the way they approach problems. It forces them to think in the same way that their peers and I will be thinking, ultimately giving everyone a good deal of alignment before the team, project, or initiative even begins. This People/Process/Product approach maintains a level of simplicity in a business environment that is growing ever more complex by the day.

I used the People, Process, and Product approach twice during my time at Mattel when confronted with significant challenges. Both times, it created stunning and very positive results. The first time was upon taking over the Girls Division at a time when the Barbie brand was struggling significantly. Sales had been down for three years in a row, competitive pressures were significant, and very talented people were struggling to make a difference. By applying this framework from the first day I began in this role, what could have been an overwhelming challenge became somewhat manageable. This framework forced me to look at the structure and team, it forced me to quickly evaluate the decision-making processes within and across the organization, and it forced a strong evaluation of what the team was delivering, including everything from the financial results to the products being introduced. None of these were easy tasks, but it was certainly easier to attack the issues once they were structured through this lens because, ultimately, I found they were all interconnected. The products being launched, for example, were not nearly as strong as those in previous years because teams were not empowered (process). Creativity and innovation were being watered down and wasted because decision making required too many people giving too much input (people). Teams were not structured with the consumer in mind, but instead were based on how division leadership wanted to manage the businesses. I could go on and on. There was no single cause of any of the problems, but a lot of little things were adding up to chaos and confusion. By framing how I attacked the issue through the Power of Three (people, process, and product) lens, the list of forty or fifty things that needed to be addressed could all ladder back to initiatives that were aligned at a strategic level. The long lists making up each section could then be prioritized based on both the impact that resolving them would have and the speed at which resolution could be achieved. Quick wins were done first and ongoing efforts to resolve longer issues would be maintained. Because the simple framework gave everyone on the team context for what was being attempted, alignment was maintained over time. I won't pretend that everything was fixed and running great when I moved on to the digital world within Mattel, but the foundation was operating significantly more effectively, allowing the talent and the creativity to overcome the process and structure challenges that will always be present in big organizations.

A second example of applying the Power of Three via the people, process, and product framework occurred when I started overseeing all things digital at Mattel. Given that it was 2008, digital was a huge area that was changing the world, and Mattel did not have a clear strategy for this area. They had many successful initiatives and ideas and some very talented people, but nothing that allowed people to work together, created synergies, and excited the organization from top to bottom.

In this instance, I assumed responsibility for many different groups within the company, web, e-commerce, mobile development, and video games being among them. Within those groups, there were various functions. People with great expertise who had never been working on a common goal or mission filled roles in those functions. Using the framework, within ninety days, the team and I were able to provide a "mission" that aligned everyone—a clear organizational structure that increased peoples' roles and scopes without sacrificing their daily responsibilities and increased the team's output using the same resources and amount of dollars. Within a year, we had completely rethought the company's web strategy, created the number-three kids' web portal in terms of traffic and visits, launched an e-commerce store that dramatically improved consumer's understanding of Mattel and its brands, initiated a social strategy for key brands, began development on our branded video games, and increased revenue generated in the digital space by 100% over the previous year. Obviously, this was a ton of progress achieved extremely quickly and efficiently and using 80% of the same people that had been working in this area for the previous few years.

Why such great progress? Simply put, by leveraging the framework of the Power of Three (people, process and product), we were able to align very quickly as a team and establish a clear understanding of how the process should work and a unified understanding of what we were expected to deliver. There were still many other issues to be worked out, but the internal team found a unified purpose that allowed us to focus on the business and not the structure or the politics of the company.

The Power of Three has also worked well in terms of framing up how I communicate to audiences, both small and large. It wasn't until I was doing many large group presentations that I realized the Power of Three principle could actually be a communication framework for everything. For large audiences, I begin by breaking the "story" or narrative into three segments. Usually the presentation starts with the context, or the "why" section of what will be shared. It moves on to a core section, or the "what and how" section, where key ideas are outlined. Finally, the third segment is a summary. Said differently, the entire presentation can be broken down as "the what," "the why," and "the how."

In looking at many different methods of teaching presentation skills or communication skills, there is a general rule to "tell them what you will say, say it, and then tell them what you said." This is very similar to what I am suggesting, and I am not sure if it even matters how you think about the segments, as long as you think about the entire presentation and frame it in three segments. The segments help your audience understand what they are about to see, makes your message memorable and easy to understand, and, most importantly, makes the presentation very simple to construct.

As stated at the beginning of the chapter, far smarter and significantly better-educated people have explored this concept much more powerfully than I have in this chapter. When you start to apply the Power of Three framework to many parts of life, you start to see a pattern. Whether it's the spiritual world (the Father, the Son, and the Holy Spirit), your personal world (yourself, your family, and your extended friends), or your work life (your boss, your staff, and your peers), you can both apply the Power of Three principle and see it playing itself out all around you.

Whether you're dealing with a "To Do" list that is simply too big and you don't know how to prioritize everything or have only one big hairy issue you are trying to resolve, the solution is the same: Step back, break it all down into an organizing framework, put the detail underneath, and see if it simplifies the challenge. The power of three can be an amazing tool to help you become more strategic, more thoughtful, and more proactive. It can help you align more quickly with teams of people by making things easier to understand. Finally, it can help you break down complex issues into simple, manageable tasks that will give you a better sense that those issues can be overcome, progress can be made, and that nothing is truly unmanageable.

CHAPTER 5

Beware of the Sofa Bed

This chapter will be short and simple because the thought is. (Although that statement does suggest the previous four chapters were filled with some form of deep and meaningful ideas.).

Let's start with the statement: "Beware of the sofa bed." This statement comes from the idea that compromise may not always be the best solution. Don't get me wrong, life is full of compromise, and it's important, but when making or designing something, it can truly be an enemy of greatness. To be more specific, if you were to ask people what they thought of sofa beds, virtually everyone would have the same reaction: "Well, it's an okay couch" or "It's an okay bed." They probably would have some memory of sleeping on a bad pull-out sofa or sitting on a lumpy couch. Regardless, I can almost assure you that you will never find someone whose memory is that a sofa bed he has experienced was either the best couch or the best bed he has ever sat or slept on. Why? Because the maker of the sofa bed had to make compromises to make the piece of furniture work and function as required. Maybe the manufacturer had to put that bar in the middle of an ultra-thin mattress to get it to fold. Maybe the unit had to be made heavier than a Toyota Prius just to make it hold up and function like both a couch and a bed. The fact is that manufacturers of sofa beds had to make compromises in function, in style, in weight, or in comfort. These compromises were necessary, and they provide a very functional piece of furniture that can serve a purpose, but the goal of making a dual-use piece of furniture and the compromises in design that were required to make it function means that it is not going to be the best solution for sleeping on every night or sitting on every day. Thankfully, companies have also realized that we need the best solution for each of those needs independently. Without the specific solutions that are designed and built just for the purpose of sitting or sleeping, we would all be uncomfortable a lot of the time.

Don't get me wrong; brilliance can come from putting two things together and creating an opportunity. I think you can see that happening with the technology impacting everything in our lives. If combining two concepts doesn't come naturally and you have to explain why you have pushed two things together, however, then admit that this is a problem, pick one, and go. One phenomenal solution to one problem is better than a mediocre solution to two problems. People don't want mediocre; people won't accept that it's "just okay," and, ultimately, they will find another alternative. People may use or accept a sofa bed occasionally, but they will ultimately look for both a great sofa *and* a great bed.

A perfect example of the sofa bed framework that I built in the toy business was the introduction of Barbie Girls back in 2007. The idea was simple—build a virtual world, known as a massively multi-player online game (an MMO), that allowed girls to create an avatar, play online with their character, chat with friends, and have a virtual fashion-doll experience. To help drive the idea, we introduced a product that looked and acted like a 3D paper doll, but was really a 3D key that served to unlock the virtual world for girls. Those girls who had this key were rewarded with a significantly larger and more engaging experience than those that logged onto the virtual world for free. Unfortunately, all of us were concerned that a key would not be enough to excite girls, because we knew we would be appealing to older girls, so we elected to add more technology into the physical toy. Specifically, we added an MP3 player, which allowed girls to also listen to their favorite music when they were away from the computer.

It sounded like a great idea, but in hindsight, what was created was an expensive sofa bed. It was a compromise composed of many ideas that lost sight of what girls really wanted. The main idea was the online experience, not the technology that we were including in the toy (the MP3 player). As a result, the Barbie Girls keys were $40 to $50 retail instead of what they could have been, $19.99. While the idea was somewhat successful in its first year and continued for another eighteen months as a great MMO for girls, the entire program would have been much more successful if we had stayed focused on the core idea of the virtual world, which could have been monetized through the low cost "key" concept. We made an amazing sofa bed with the introduction of Barbie Girls, but found out that girls didn't want a sofa bed. Girls wanted a singular online experience that was unique, engaging, and fun, not a mash-up of two good ideas trying to be one "ultimate" idea.

Again, it's easy to see it after the fact. Just make sure that as you strive to deliver a product or service, you do it with a singular focus. Pick one thing to be great at and do not waver. This focus, this unwavering determination to be great at something, will prevent you from creating a "sofa bed" and delivering mediocrity

CHAPTER 6

The Difference between Consensus and Collaboration

Okay, this one can sound like semantics, and I honestly don't think I realized or appreciated this concept until recently. Knowing the difference between consensus and collaboration has become a fundamental insight that I focus upon when working with teams. I have found that it is a lot tougher to accomplish than it sounds. Simply put, the difference between consensus and collaboration is massive and can be the difference between success and failure on any given project.

In looking at organizations in which I have been involved, these two words are often used interchangeably, but the meanings of these two words are not even close. Webster's Dictionary defines each as follows:

Consensus: a general agreement; group solidarity in sentiment and belief.

Collaboration: to work jointly with others in an especially intellectual endeavor; to cooperate with or willingly assist.

As seen in these definitions, the difference between the two words is dramatic. The first is about agreement, and the second is about working together. Yet, in many organizations I have worked with and seen, these words are used interchangeably and, very often, incorrectly.

It's important to know that there is a time and place for both consensus and collaboration. There are many things we decide and do every day in which consensus is the perfectly correct method for resolving the question at hand: Where do you go to lunch? What time do you meet for drinks? How do we resolve a simple problem and move forward? It's about gaining alignment and, in most circumstances, it's easy to do. There are no critical or urgent things to resolve that require emotional discussions or arguments. The group talks, they accept a decision, and they move forward. There are no issues, and all is good. In these circumstances, it becomes more about finding the lowest common denominator for agreement than about pushing and finding the best solution, because that is all that is required, but if teams are faced with challenges in which change is needed and progress must be significant, using consensus instead of collaboration can be a dangerous mistake.

Collaboration is about working together to drive significant change and progress. It is not only about aligning, but also about establishing a purpose and a goal to drive significant change, about creating something truly inspirational and exciting, and about achieving more as a group than any one individual alone could. It is about listening to all points of view, both positive and negative, and not settling for a solution, but stretching to achieve a much bigger idea than anyone thought possible at the beginning of the discussion.

When I think about consensus versus collaboration, I honestly see a simple picture in my head:

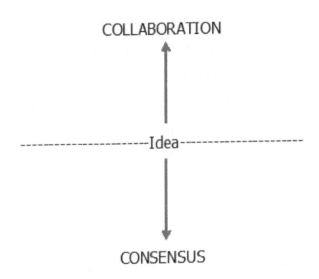

Simply put, collaboration is about taking an idea, usually a good one with a few flaws or issues, addressing those flaws and issues, and delivering an even better idea that has significantly improved the original idea. Consensus, on the other hand, is about taking an idea, watering it down to a point where no one complains, and calling that a resolution.

I will say that collaboration is a learned skill, and one that not everyone is born to do well. Some people are very comfortable getting feedback and working to adjust their thinking, while others simply want everyone to agree to the their idea. It's the difference between working to make the best solution and working to get a task done. The first is truly trying to do what is best, while the second is about getting finished.

I will leave you with two real-life examples to better understand the difference between consensus and collaboration. The first example focuses on how to facilitate collaboration and make it happen. The second example illustrates an instance in which collaboration happens all the time and no one realizes it.

On facilitating collaboration, it starts with an easy action or requirement of all team members.

As teams review ideas and thinking, all participants must acknowledge points that they like about ideas being expressed before articulating any concerns. Whether the positive feedback is about the entire idea or something very trivial doesn't matter. Those providing feedback must start with the positive. Obviously, the more trivial the feedback is (e.g., "I like the PowerPoint template"), the more likely a difficult and courageous conversation will be following. By starting with positive feedback, however, you immediately build a bridge to the presenter or owner of the initial thought. Given that this person felt strongly enough to express their point of view about what needs to be done, it's the team's job to make that work and make that person feel appreciated.

The idea presenter or generator also has a critical role to play. Their role is two-fold—they must receive the feedback without taking it personally, and, more importantly, as they begin to express their thinking, it is critical that they establish the context for the issue and state why they believe it to be important. This focus on context is important because regardless of the solution provided, if there is agreement on the issue that must be resolved, alignment over something important has already been achieved. For perspective, I have seen many teams align on the overall issue, but there was no alignment on the proposed solution. This is okay, because even gaining agreement on an important issue is a critical step. By aligning at this most upfront stage, you can ensure that the team is focused on the problem (the disease) and not arguing about the solution (the symptom).

As for the example in which collaboration happens all the time, I would highlight the brainstorming process. Brainstorming, by its nature, allows people to be creative, to work together, and to have some fun. These moments are seen as truly energizing, because a brainstorm is rooted in collaboration. The first idea spurs another, and then another, and ideas are almost never shot down or critiqued. Brainstorms, by their very nature, are select moments when people are building off the ideas of each other in a way that doesn't assign credit (or blame) to any one person, but elevates the team output over the individual. The ideation that results from one idea building to another is incredibly positive and almost never gets into the "why something won't work" phase. Instead, the common goal and supportive environment give everyone a sense of camaraderie, teamwork, and purpose that simply doesn't exist in the day-to-day approach to a job.

Recognize when to use collaboration instead of consensus. Collaboration drives significant progress and truly leads to better thinking than any individual can do alone. More importantly, don't give in to consensus when collaboration is what is needed.

CHAPTER 7

Are You Focused on What You're Selling or Making?

This thought has only recently become clear to me, but it has become a very important organizing thought or principle in terms of how to think about a company or business. From a business perspective, it has become very powerful in challenging situations.

The simple thought is that every company must focus on what it sells, not what it makes. The distinction between the two words doesn't sound like much, but the difference is huge, because it gets at the heart of what your customers are buying from you and not what you are making. Let me see if I can better explain what I am talking about through a few examples:

Let's start with Kodak. Kodak was the world's leader in film and is still considered by many to be the preeminent name in photography. It is one of the world's best-known brands. However, if you look at Kodak today, the company is a shell of what it once was, having declared bankruptcy and tried to sell off patents to raise money. Its decline is the result of the film business dropping significantly as digital photography became the world standard. I recognize that many companies don't see the future, but the scary thing about Kodak is that it didn't miss the digital trend—at least from a Research & Development perspective. It is well documented that a Kodak engineer actually developed the first digital camera; most cameras today have elements that license a Kodak patent for digital photography. When the company was presented with the idea back in the 1970s, the engineer was told, "We are in the film business, not the camera business." To look back and think that Kodak was there first, but didn't see it, is amazing. Without question, it was the single biggest moment responsible for their recent difficulties.

Had the Kodak leadership at the time looked through the lens of what people were buying versus what Kodak was making, the company would have realized that people bought Kodak film to capture memories. These memories might be served up in the form of pictures and delivered via film, but ultimately, people were trusting Kodak to capture memories. The fact is that the average consumer didn't care whether memories were captured on film or digitally; they just wanted to protect the special moments. Kodak's entire value chain had been built on film; building after building and person after person in the company were focused on film. This focus, while important for day-to-day operations back in the '70s, meant that the Kodak digital camera went back on the shelf. The future was set at that moment. Today, Kodak is just one of many camera and photo companies because it didn't recognize the true focus of what it was selling and what consumers were really buying.

The second example of missing an opportunity because a company is focused on what it made instead of what people were buying is Blockbuster Video. Blockbuster was a truly extraordinary company that changed the way the world watched movies at home. It took a very fragmented category (think of all the mom-and-pop video rental stores of the late '80's and early '90's) and created an entertainment powerhouse. Blockbuster offered a bigger selection, more early releases, and consistent quality. The list of improvements goes on and on. Blockbuster addressed any issue that seemed to be a problem for small stores. It can even be said that Blockbuster accelerated the consumer shift to DVDs simply by discontinuing support of VHS tapes. There was no other company focused on home entertainment that was even close. Blockbuster owned the DVD rental business.

Here again, we will see the "sell versus make" thought play itself out. We will see where Blockbuster was truly blind to the marketplace. Blockbuster was in the business of DVD rentals. This is what they "made." Therefore, Blockbuster's strategy was focused on DVD distribution, which translated into building stores, increasing their real-estate holdings, and adding more titles to the wall of movies. What consumers were "buying" was a convenient way to bring movies into their homes. They didn't care how they got the movie; they just wanted to have time with their families in the most convenient, cost-effective way possible. See the big disconnect? Blockbuster is selling "DVD rentals," building an entire value chain of retail stores and distribution behind the DVD rental business. Consumers were buying convenient home entertainment.

Along comes a company called Netflix, which understood that consumers were buying convenient home entertainment. People didn't care how the movie was delivered, as along at the company improved on the convenience while competing equally or better on title selection and value. Netflix started to change the game by not having stores (which was the biggest advantage offered by Blockbuster), instead focusing on seamless delivery of the DVDs to the end consumer via the mail. Simultaneously, Netflix invested heavily into streaming technology, which now allows them to send movies to a consumer's home instantly over the Internet. The end result is that Netflix can now improve the consumer experience (no waiting or driving to get a movie), deliver this experience for less cost, and avoid having a cost structure that has to support thousands of retail stores.

Making matters worse for Blockbuster, a new startup (Redbox) realized that while streaming was fine, there was still a market for that last-minute movie rental, but delivered via vending machines instead of stores. In this model, a consumer can rent movies for a dollar, eliminating the need for real estate, employees, and general overhead, and the company can locate the machines everywhere so that consumers don't have to make another stop. All of a sudden, Blockbuster found itself being squeezed on both sides, with Netflix owning convenience and delivery and Redbox owning a different form of convenience, as well as great value. It is this perfect storm of competitive pressures that progressed to the point at which Blockbuster declared bankruptcy and ended up being purchased for pennies on the dollar by Direct TV. Putting it bluntly, Blockbuster never understood that what it sold was convenient home entertainment for a good value. Instead, it got caught up in how many stores were in each city and how many titles were on each wall. Blockbuster never got its head around what it was selling versus what it was making.

The final example of companies focused on the wrong side of the equation is found in the music industry. For years, the record companies were in the CD distribution business. As the Web exploded and digital music became more mainstream, the music industry fought this change from not dealing with digital rights management to suing consumers who were using file-sharing software. (It doesn't take a business genius to know that it can never be a good long-term strategy to sue your end consumer.) The music companies simply refused to deal with the problem. Simply put, music companies saw themselves in the CD/music distribution business while consumers were buying music.

Along came Apple, who just wanted to sell music. They didn't care how it was made, distributed, or packaged. Apple could see that people were buying music, not CDs. Apple also realized that sometimes people wanted to buy one song, and other times, the entire album. If you were in the business of distributing CDs, and that was your entire business model, you might have known these were issues, but you were prepared to fight that shift as long as you could because your company and everything you did was structured around making and shipping CDs. If you were Apple, you responded to what people were buying, changed the delivery system by launching iTunes, and fundamentally changed the music industry forever.

Each of these stories and examples has a lot more depth, detail, and learning than I have shared in this short chapter. I can also guarantee that if someone were to look at the last twenty years of my career, there have been plenty of occasions in which I focused on what my company was making versus what was selling. The point is, however, that by using this frame at the front end of an issue or challenge, it can truly help you to think in a new way. It will force you to not get caught up in what the company does, but instead focus on the real purpose of your company and why people are buying your products or services now. It isn't easy to do, but it should help you to drive significant and important change that is critical for your company's future.

One final thought that I will leave you with on this topic is that the actions that you and your company make today are likely in place because that is what has been successful in the past, but it's also very likely that this may not be the right thing to continue in order to be successful in the future. If you are not challenging these things, there is a good chance that you are basing your future on the hope that nothing changes in your industry or category and, as discussed before, hope shouldn't be the foundation of your plans going forward.

CHAPTER 8

Don't Be the Smartest Person in the Room

People who have worked with me over the years know that I use this phrase when I am getting frustrated, and it's a phrase that I wanted to share because I think most people who have worked with teams of people can relate. "Don't be the smartest one in the room" relates to that time and that place when you are out of sync with those with whom you are working. It might be a team, a peer group, or company management—it really doesn't matter. It's that feeling that you are the only one with new ideas, the one who is thinking more clearly than others, the one who seems to be the "only one who gets it." Suffice it to say, you are wrong. You are not the only one who gets it, the only one with new ideas, or the only one thinking clearly. It simply means that you are significantly disconnected from your peers and your company, and it's that disconnect that is giving you that feeling. Let me try and be more specific:

Feeling disconnected from your company or your peers is natural. It happens, and as long as it's not happening all the time, it's not a bad thing. It may be that you are having a bad week, it may be that you don't have all the background or details on the project, or it may mean that you are actually way ahead of the other folks involved, seeing things before they do and anticipating things that need to be done. Who knows why the disconnect happens? It just does. If, however, it goes on and on for an extended and consistent period of time, it may be time to think about the underlying cause, because there is a high likelihood that this feeling is more about you than the company or your peers.

I have found myself with this prolonged feeling of being disconnected twice in my career. The first was after two years at a sports equipment company, and the second was at the end of my eighteen years at Mattel. As I look back at both of the times where I felt like the "smartest," I can now say with confidence that both instances had nothing to do with me being smarter than everyone else. (If you have made it through this book or know me personally, it's likely that you arrived at this same conclusion a number of pages earlier.) Instead, I believe this feeling can be directly related to the simple ideas that I could no longer agree with the decisions being made *and* I could no longer understand why the decisions were being enacted. Put another way, there have been many times in which I didn't agree with a decision, but I understood why we needed to make it. There were other times in which I could agree with a decision, even if I didn't fully understand why it was being made. It was when I found myself in a position in which I both didn't agree with a decision and could not understand why an action was needed that I found myself feeling like the "smartest."

In those instances, when I found myself not only disagreeing with decisions but also confused by how anyone had come to see this decision as the best path forward, I felt "smarter" than everyone else and disconnected in a very real sense. I also realized that given my very senior role, this disconnect was consistently occurring during discussions and work focused on the future path and direction of the company. When I could neither agree with nor understand what was happening, I could no longer give the company my best. When I came to this "smartest in the room" realization over an extended period of time, it both gave me pause to rethink what I was doing and, more importantly, spurred me to action because something needed to change. In both instances, I made the change I felt was necessary and that I felt I could control. Right or wrong, I fundamentally believed it was both the best thing for me and for the company, and, as I have often joked with former team members, "I couldn't sit in the corner and bitch about management when I was management." I simply could not be the best leader because of how I was feeling, and the folks who worked for me deserved someone who wasn't conflicted about where things were going.

This idea and the corresponding implications is not something that can be broadly discussed. It is very personal and different for every person, but I do encourage you to think about these moments and try to get to the heart of why you are feeling that way.

Summary

As I finish this book, I hope that I have accomplished what I set out to do—to create a simple read that gives you something to think about as you go about your life. Whether it's your personal life or your work life, I hope that a lot of these thoughts and frameworks can apply to the challenges you face every day. Do not let hope become your *de facto* strategy. Simplify the complex issues into actions by using these and other frameworks that help you feel more in control and less reactive to whatever situation you are facing.

Thank you for taking the time to read this, and I sincerely hope these frameworks will help you as they have helped me.

Acknowledgements

There are many thank-yous that I owe to people who have helped me over the years, so let's get started.

To anyone that may see some of these thoughts as yours: If they are, thank you, and I apologize if you feel I borrowed anything. I have done my best to make each of the ideas shared here frameworks that I have used throughout my life and career.

To all that I have worked with, both those that I worked well with and those that I didn't work well with, thank you. Either way, you taught me a lot about myself and about teamwork.

To Chuck R, who said it best one day while giving me some constructive feedback: "Stop whining and quit being the victim." You were right.

To Neil: Not many would have had the confidence to turn over a brand like Fisher Price to someone who was only thirty-seven. Your ability to know when to get involved and when to let people go their own way taught me much, and your willingness to both trust people and allow them to make mistakes is something that everyone should learn. Thank you.

To Jerry: You saw something in me that others didn't (especially when I was twenty-four years old and days away from being fired), and for that, I will always be thankful. You are not just a friend, but someone who inspires me. Your ability to see the good in every situation is something I aspire to live by. Thank you.

To my friends at Fisher Price: To all that I worked with and grew up with, from design to marketing to every department in the company, I just want to say thanks. I'm not sure I understood the power of collaboration until I worked with all of you. Thank you.

To my Mattel Friends: You taught me that smarts, guts, and intuition can make all the difference. Embrace the idea of "Creating the Future of Play." Thank you.

To my parents: You taught me so much and gave me such opportunity. Some things I learned from you, and some I learned from what you made me do. Either way, I am better and smarter for it. Thank you, and I love you.

To Gabriella: Find your passion in life and make it your life's work. I found that I love working with people and leading teams, and somehow, this book is one of the results. Once you find what inspires you, your very sweet spirit and amazing heart will shine through. Thank you for inspiring me every day.

To Annette: I don't know where to start. From challenging me to accomplish more to supporting my decision to leave Mattel and take a flying leap without a clear plan, you are amazing. Even if I was successful in business, I wouldn't be successful in life if it wasn't for you. Thank you for your love, your heart, and being you. I love you more than you will ever know!